THE LIFE OF THE VIRGIN MARY

ζάλην ἔνδοθεν ἔχων
[*Having a storm within*]

RAINER MARIA RILKE

➤➤➤➤➤➤➤➤◄◄◄◄◄◄◄◄

THE LIFE OF THE
VIRGIN MARY

TRANSLATED, WITH AN INTRODUCTION AND NOTES, BY

C. F. MacINTYRE

GREENWOOD PRESS, PUBLISHERS
WESTPORT, CONNECTICUT

The Library of Congress has catalogued this publication as follows:

Library of Congress Cataloging in Publication Data

Rilke, Rainer Maria, 1875-1926.
    The life of the Virgin Mary.

    German and English on opposite pages.
    Translation of Das Marienleben.
    Includes bibliographical references.
    1. Mary, Virgin—Poetry. I. Title.
[PT2635.I65M35 1972]   831'.9'12   74-138178
ISBN 0-8371-5635-1

Originally published in 1947
by University of California Press

Reprinted with the permission
of Philosophical Library, New York

Reprinted from an original copy in the collections
of the University of Illinois Library

First Greenwood Reprinting 1972

Library of Congress Catalogue Card Number 74-138178

ISBN 0-8371-5635-1

Printed in the United States of America

TO
MY SECOND MOTHER
CHARLOTTA
A MOST CONSISTENT CATHOLIC

PREFACE

Perhaps the validity of the originals of these translations will be found to lie in the warmly human treatment with which Rilke has presented his characters. Here he resembles the painters of the Middle Ages. For instance, in the first poem is the officious and ignorant old woman from next door who wants to be helpful; and there is fine understanding of man's futility, on such occasions, in Joachim's attempt to do something, however useless. The need of the pregnant women to be near and to touch each other, Joseph's doubts and his ready conviction when the angel speaks in the carpenter's own terms, Mary's pride in her son's triumphs and her motherly desire to show him off, her utter desolation at his death, and her disposal of her clothes before her own death—these are shining examples of the poet's wisdom in the ways of human beings and of his simple dramatic presentation of their actions.

The Life of the Virgin Mary was begun in 1900, under the inspiration of some sketches by Heinrich Vögler. It was rewritten and published in 1913, with a dedication to the artist, but the drawings were not included in the book.

The poems, appearing midway in Rilke's work, lie somewhat apart from the main course of his development. They have more relation to his earlier descriptive verse, the imitation folk songs, and to those pious versicles done under a false Russian stimulation, the *Book of Hours,* than to the melancholy lyrics of the *Book of Pictures,* the sophisticated, 'parnassian' *New Poems,* and the culmination of his work in the powerful and mystic *Duino Elegies* and their by-product the *Sonnets to Orpheus.*

Whether or not Rilke was an orthodox Catholic has no bearing on the effect of the series as poetry—the immediate communication and the sincerity of the impression. And it is because the other great poets of the last hundred years, including Baudelaire, Mallarmé, Stefan George, and Paul Valéry—but leaving aside Claudel and Péguy, and Gerard Manley Hopkins,—have ignored the Bible as a source of subject matter, Rilke's delicate contribution to the tradition may seem especially significant and unusual.

For critical suggestions and advice I am much indebted to Professor Edward V. Brewer, of the University of California, and Professor B. Q. Morgan, of Stanford University.

C.F.M.

CONTENTS

CONTENTS

DAS MARIENLEBEN

GEBURT MARIÄ

O was muss es die Engel gekostet haben,
nicht aufzusingen plötzlich, wie man aufweint,
da sie doch wussten: in dieser Nacht wird dem Knaben
die Mutter geboren, dem Einen, der bald erscheint.

Schwingend verschwiegen sie sich und zeigten die Richtung,
wo, allein, das Gehöft lag des Joachim,
ach, sie fühlten in sich und im Raum die reine Verdichtung,
aber es durfte keiner nieder zu ihm.

Denn die beiden waren schon so ausser sich vor Getue.
Eine Nachbarin kam und klugte und wusste nicht wie,
und der Alte, vorsichtig, ging und verhielt das Gemuhe
einer dunkelen Kuh. Denn so war es noch nie.

BIRTH OF MARY

Oh, what must it have cost the angels not
to sing out suddenly, as one bursts in tears,
since they well knew: the mother is born tonight
who bears the boy, the One who will soon appear.

Hovering, they kept silence and showed the way
down which Joachim's lonely homestead lay;
ah, they felt pure tension in themselves, in the air,
but no one might go down to him. The pair

were already out of their wits with what was doing.
A neighbor came and played wise but didn't know how.
The old man went and stopped the dark cow's mooing,
thoughtfully. Such a night never was till now.

DIE DARSTELLUNG MARIÄ IM TEMPEL

Um zu begreifen, wie sie damals war,
musst du dich erst an eine Stelle rufen,
wo Säulen in dir wirken; wo du Stufen
nachfühlen kannst; wo Bogen voll Gefahr
den Abgrund eines Raumes überbrücken,
der in dir blieb, weil er aus solchen Stücken
getürmt war, dass du sie nicht mehr aus dir
ausheben kannst: du rissest dich denn ein.
Bist du so weit, ist alles in dir Stein,
Wand, Aufgang, Durchblick, Wölbung—, so probier,
den grossen Vorhang, den du vor dir hast,
ein wenig wegzuzerrn mit beiden Händen:
Da glänzt es von ganz hohen Gegenständen
und übertrifft dir Atem und Getast.
Hinauf, hinab, Palast sieht auf Palast,
Geländer strömen breiter aus Geländern
und tauchen oben auf an solchen Rändern,
dass dich, wie du sie siehst, der Schwindel fasst.
Dabei macht ein Gewölk aus Räucherständern
die Nähe trüb; aber das Fernste zielt
in dich hinein mit seinen graden Strahlen—,
und wenn jetzt Schein aus klaren Flammenschalen
auf langsam nahenden Gewändern spielt:
wie hälst du's aus?

(Continued on page 6)

[4]

THE PRESENTATION OF MARY
IN THE TEMPLE

To comprehend how she was at that time,
you must first imagine yourself in a place
where pillars work within you, where you climb
the stairs and feel the steps, where the deep space
of a chasm bridged with arches full of peril
remained in you because it had been piled
of fragments which you can no longer raise
lest you tear down yourself. If you have gone
so far that all in you is wall and stone,
stairway, vista, vaulting—try
with both your hands to drag aside the curtain
so heavy there before you, just a bit:
a glory flashes from the infinite
and overcomes your breath and numbs your touch.
Palace looks on palace from depth to heights;
from balustrades stream broader balustrades,
emerging above such verges that the sight
grows dizzy, gazing, and you are afraid.
Near-by the censers nebulously shade
the air with murk; but level rays
are aimed at you from the most distant space,
and if on slowly nearing vestments plays
radiance from vessels of clear flame,
how will you bear it?

(Continued on page 7)

DIE DARSTELLUNG MARIÄ
IM TEMPEL—*Continued*

Sie aber kam und hob
den Blick, um dieses alles anzuschauen.
(Ein Kind, ein kleines Mädchen zwischen Frauen.)
Dann stieg sie ruhig, voller Selbstvertrauen,
dem Aufwand zu, der sich verwöhnt verschob:
So sehr war alles, was die Menschen bauen,
schon überwogen von dem Lob

in ihrem Herzen. Von der Lust
sich hinzugeben an die innern Zeichen:
Die Eltern meinten, sie hinaufzureichen,
der Drohende mit der Juwelenbrust
empfing sie scheinbar: Doch sie ging durch alle,
klein wie sie war, aus jeder Hand hinaus
und in ihr Los, das, höher als die Halle,
schon fertig war, und schwerer als das Haus.

THE PRESENTATION OF MARY
IN THE TEMPLE—*Continued*

But she came and raised
her eyes and looked at all of this. (Though just
a child, a small girl among women.) Then
she mounted calmly, full of her self-trust,
toward a pomp that fastidiously gave way—
so much was everything that men
build already outweighed by the praise

within her heart. She so yearned
to give herself up to the inner signs —
her parents had intended to present her —
the threatening one on whose breast jewels burned
seemed to receive her; but she passed through all,
small as she was, forth from every hand,
into her destiny prepared, more ample
than the hall and heavier than the temple.

MARIÄ VERKÜNDIGUNG

NICHT dass ein Engel eintrat (das erkenn),
erschreckte sie. So wenig andre, wenn
ein Sonnenstrahl oder der Mond bei Nacht
in ihrem Zimmer sich zu schaffen macht,
auffahren—, pflegte sie an der Gestalt,
in der ein Engel ging, sich zu entrüsten;
sie ahnte kaum, dass dieser Aufenthalt
mühsam für Engel ist. (O wenn wir wüssten,
wie rein sie war. Hat eine Hirschkuh nicht,
die, liegend, einmal sie im Wald eräugte,
sich so in sie versehn, dass sich in ihr,
ganz ohne Paarigen, das Einhorn zeugte,
das Tier aus Licht, das reine Tier—.)
Nicht, dass er eintrat, aber dass er dicht,
der Engel, eines Jünglings Angesicht
so zu ihr neigte, dass sein Blick und der,
mit dem sie aufsah, so zusammenschlugen,
als wäre draussen plötzlich alles leer
und, was Millionen schauten, trieben, trugen,
hineingedrängt in sie: nur sie und er;
Schaun und Geschautes, Aug und Augenweide
sonst nirgends als an dieser Stelle—: sieh,
dieses erschreckt. Und sie erschraken beide.

Dann sang der Engel seine Melodie.

ANNUNCIATION TO MARY

Nor that an angel came in, understand,
was she alarmed. As little as others start
when a sunray or beam of moonlight darts
into a room and busies itself here and there,
would she have been made angry by the guise
in which an angel came. Could she surmise
how tedious angels find such tarrying here?
(Oh, if we knew how pure she was! A hind,
once when resting, saw her in the wood,
and gazing lost itself until it could —
all without any coupling with its kind —
conceive the unicorn, pure animal,
the beast of light.) Not that he entered, but
that he bowed down so close to her the face
of a young man, this angel, that her gaze
as she glanced up joined with his, as if all
outside there suddenly seemed void and what
the millions saw, were doing, suffering,
seemed forced into them: only she and he—
the seeing and seen, the eye and eye's delight
nowhere else but in this one place. See!
this is frightening. And they were both afraid.

Then the angel sang his melody.

MARIÄ HEIMSUCHUNG

Noch erging sie's leicht im Anbeginne,
doch im Steigen manchmal ward sie schon
ihres wunderbaren Leibes inne, —
und dann stand sie, atmend, auf den hohn

Judenbergen. Aber nicht das Land,
ihre Fülle war um sie gebreitet;
gehend fühlte sie: man überschreitet
nie die Grösse, die sie jetzt empfand.

Und es drängte sie, die Hand zu legen
auf den andern Leib, der weiter war.
Und die Frauen schwankten sich entgegen
und berührten sich Gewand und Haar.

Jede, voll von ihrem Heiligtume,
schützte sich mit der Gevatterin.
Ach der Heiland in ihr war noch Blume,
doch den Täufer in dem Schoos der Muhme
riss die Freude schon zum Hüpfen hin.

VISITATION OF THE VIRGIN

At first it all went easily with her,
but oftentimes in climbing she already
felt the wonder stirring in her body —
and panting then she stood upon the lofty

Judean hills. Not by the land below,
she was encompassed by her plenitude;
walking, she felt that no one ever could
surpass the bigness she was feeling now.

She had to lay her hand upon the other
woman's body, still more ripe than hers.
And they both tottered toward one another
and touched each other's garments and hair.

Each, with a sanctuary in her keeping,
sought refuge with her closest woman kin.
Ah, the Savior in her was just in bloom,
but joy already in her cousin's womb
had quickened the little Baptist into leaping.

ARGWOHN JOSEPHS

Und der Engel sprach und gab sich Müh
an dem Mann, der seine Fäuste ballte:
Aber siehst du nicht an jeder Falte,
dass sie kühl ist wie die Gottesfrüh.

Doch der andre sah ihn finster an,
murmelnd nur: Was hat sie so verwandelt?
Doch da schrie der Engel: Zimmermann,
merkst du's noch nicht, dass der Herrgott handelt?

Weil du Bretter machst, in deinem Stolze,
willst du wirklich den zur Rede stelln,
der bescheiden aus dem gleichen Holze
Blätter treiben macht und Knospen schwelln?

Er begriff. Und wie er jetzt die Blicke,
recht erschrocken, zu dem Engel hob,
war der fort. Da schob er seine dicke
Mütze langsam ab. Dann sang er lob.

JOSEPH'S SUSPICION

AND the angel, taking due pains, told
the man who clenched his fists:
But can't you see in her robe's every fold
that she is cool as the Lord's morning mists?

But the other, gazing gloomily, just murmured:
What is it has wrought this change in her?
Then cried the angel to him: Carpenter,
can't you see yet that God is acting here?

Because you plane the planks, in your pride would
you really make the Lord God answerable
who unpretentiously from the same wood
makes the leaves burst forth, the young buds swell?

He understood that. And now as he raised
his frightened glance toward the angel who
was gone already . . . slowly the man drew
his heavy cap off. Then in song he praised.

VERKÜNDIGUNG ÜBER DEN HIRTEN

SEHT auf, ihr Männer. Männer dort am Feuer,
die ihr den grenzenlosen Himmel kennt,
Sterndeuter, hierher! Seht, ich bin ein neuer
steigender Stern. Mein ganzes Wesen brennt
und strahlt so stark und ist so ungeheuer
voll Licht, dass mir das tiefe Firmament
nicht mehr genügt. Lasst meinen Glanz hinein
in euer Dasein: o, die dunklen Blicke,
die dunklen Herzen, nächtige Geschicke,
die euch erfüllen. Hirten, wie allein
bin ich in euch. Auf einmal wird mir Raum.
Stauntet ihr nicht: der grosse Brotfruchtbaum
warf einen Schatten. Ja, das kam von mir.
Ihr Unerschrockenen, o wüsstet ihr,
wie jetzt auf eurem schauenden Gesichte
die Zukunft scheint. In diesem starken Lichte
wird viel geschehen. Euch vertrau ichs, denn
ihr seid verschwiegen; euch Gradgläubigen
redet hier alles. Glut und Regen spricht,
der Vögel Zug, der Wind und was ihr seid,
keins überwiegt und wächst zur Eitelkeit
sich mästend an. Ihr haltet nicht
die Dinge auf im Zwischenraum der Brust,
um sie zu quälen. So wie seine Lust
durch einen Engel strömt, so treibt durch euch

(Continued on page 16)

ANNUNCIATION ABOVE THE SHEPHERDS

Look up, you men. Men there about the fire,
you who know the boundlessness of skies,
star-kenners, here! Behold, I am a star,
ascending, new. My being burns so bright
and is so overwhelmingly filled with light,
that the deep firmament can no more suffice.
Let my radiance into you. Oh, gloom
of hearts, dark looks, the destinies like night
that fill you. Shepherds, how alone I come
into you. Of a sudden there is room.
Weren't you astonished? The great breadfruit tree
cast a shadow. Yea, that came from me.
You, the unafraid, if you could know
how the future's shining even now
on your upgazing faces. Much will come
to pass in this strong light. I will trust you
with it, for you are close-mouthed. Unto true
believers all things speak here. Fire and rain,
the flight of birds, the wind, and what you are—
all speak, none predominant, growing vain,
battening itself. You do not constrain
the Things within the breast's interstices
to torture them. Even as his bliss
streams through an angel, earthly ecstasies

(Continued on page 17)

VERKÜNDIGUNG ÜBER DEN HIRTEN
(Continued)

das Irdische. Und wenn ein Dorngesträuch
aufflammte plötzlich, dürfte noch aus ihm
der Ewige euch rufen, Cherubim,
wenn sie geruhten neben eurer Herde
einherzuschreiten, wunderten euch nicht:
ihr stürztet euch auf euer Angesicht,
betetet an und nenntet dies die Erde.

Doch dieses war. Nun soll ein neues sein,
von dem der Erdkreis ringender sich weitet.
Was ist ein Dörnicht uns: Gott fühlt sich ein
in einer Jungfrau Schooss. Ich bin der Schein
von ihrer Innigkeit, der euch geleitet.

ANNUNCIATION ABOVE THE SHEPHERDS
(Continued)

penetrate you. Should a thornbush flame,
out of which the Eternal Himself might call,
and if the cherubim should deign
to walk by your flock, you'd marvel not at all,
but throw yourselves down, worshiping, and call

this earth. Such things have been. Now something new
shall be to make earth whirl through wider room.
What's a thornbush to us? The Lord
feels Himself into a virgin's womb.
I am the bright recórd
of her deep fervor, I who go with you.

GEBURT CHRISTI

Hättest du der Einfalt nicht, wie sollte
dir geschehn, was jetzt die Nacht erhellt?
Sieh, der Gott, der über Völker grollte,
macht sich mild und kommt in dir zur Welt.

Hast du dir ihn grösser vorgestellt?

Was ist Grösse? Quer durch alle Masse,
die er durchstreicht, geht sein grades Los.
Selbst ein Stern hat keine solche Strasse,
siehst du, diese Könige sind gross,

und sie schleppen dir vor deinen Schooss

Schätze, die sie für die grössten halten,
und du staunst vielleicht bei dieser Gift—:
aber schau in deines Tuches Falten,
wie er jetzt schon alles übertrifft.

Aller Amber, den man weit verschifft,

jeder Goldschmuck und das Luftgewürze,
das sich trübend in die Sinne streut:
alles dieses war von rascher Kürze,
und am Ende hat man es bereut.

Aber (du wirst sehen): Er erfreut.

BIRTH OF CHRIST

Had you not simplicity, then how
should this befall you which illumines the night?
The god, who thundered above the peoples, now
makes himself mild and comes in you to light

the world. Did you imagine him as greater?

What is greatness? Straightway through all matter
where he passes moves his downright fate.
Even a star has no such highway. See,
these kings are great.

They drag before your lap

treasures which they deem the very greatest,
and you're astonished at these gifts perhaps—
but see here in the foldings of your shawl
how he already has surpassed them all.

All amber that ships carry far away,

the golden ornaments and overcloying
spices stealing in the senses: yet
all these were fleeting things that made no stay,
and finally one has little but regret.

But—you will soon know it—He brings joy.

RAST AUF DER FLUCHT IN ÄGYPTEN

DIESE, die noch eben atemlos
flohen mitten aus dem Kindermorden:
o, wie waren sie unmerklich gross
über ihrer Wanderschaft geworden.

Kaum noch dass im scheuen Rückwärtsschauen
ihres Schreckens Not zergangen war,
und schon brachten sie auf ihrem grauen
Maultier ganze Städte in Gefahr;

denn sowie sie, klein im grossen Land,
—fast ein Nichts—den starken Tempeln nahten,
platzten alle Götzen wie verraten
und verloren völlig den Verstand.

Ist es denkbar, dass von ihrem Gange
alles so verzweifelt sich erbost?
Und sie wurden vor sich selber bange,
nur das Kind war namenlos getrost.

(*Continued on page 22*)

REST ON THE FLIGHT INTO EGYPT

These who breathlessly even now were fleeing
from the slaughter of the innocents,
oh, how unnoticeably the events
of their wandering had made great their being.

But scarcely as they looked back fearfully
had the misery of their terror been forgot,
and even now on the gray mule they brought
whole mighty cities into jeopardy.

For when they, humble folk in a great land—
almost a nothing—drew near the strong temples,
all the images, as if betrayed,
crashed to earth and lost their worth as symbols.

Is it conceivable that when they passed
all things grew so furious with despair?
And they were fearful of themselves at last,
only the child was mightily of good cheer.

(Continued on page 23)

RAST AUF DER FLUCHT IN ÄGYPTEN
(Continued)

Immerhin, sie mussten sich darüber
eine Weile setzen. Doch da ging—
sieh: der Baum, der still sie überhing,
wie ein Dienender zu ihnen über:

er verneigte sich. Derselbe Baum,
dessen Kränze toten Pharaonen
für das Ewige die Stirnen schonen,
neigte sich. Er fühlte neue Kronen
blühen. Und sie sassen wie im Traum.

REST ON THE FLIGHT INTO EGYPT
(Continued)

Always because of this a little span
they had to sit and rest. But over them,
behold, the quiet tree bent on its stem
and came unto them like a servingman:

it bowed. The very tree
that guards dead Pharaohs' brow eternally
with garlands, it bent down.
It felt the new crowns bloom.
And they below sat rapt as in a dream.

VON DER HOCHZEIT ZU KANA

Konnte sie denn anders, als auf ihn
stolz sein, der ihr Schlichtestes verschönte?
War nicht selbst die hohe, grossgewöhnte
Nacht wie ausser sich, da er erschien?

Ging nicht auch, dass er sich einst verloren,
unerhört zu seiner Glorie aus?
Hatten nicht die Weisesten die Ohren
mit dem Mund vertauscht? Und war das Haus

nicht wie neu von seiner Stimme? Ach,
sicher hatte sie zu hundert Malen
ihre Freude an ihm auszustrahlen
sich verwehrt. Sie ging ihm staunend nach.

Aber da bei jenem Hochzeitsfeste,
als es unversehns an Wein gebrach,—
sah sie hin und bat um eine Geste
und begriff nicht, dass er widersprach.

Und dann tat ers. Sie verstand es später,
wie sie ihn in seinen Weg gedrängt:
denn jetzt war er wirklich Wundertäter,
und das ganze Opfer war verhängt,

(Continued on page 26)

OF THE WEDDING AT CANA

How could she but be proud of him who wrought
the simplest things more beautifully for her?
Was not even majestic night distraught,
the night used to so much, when he appeared?

And even that time when he was lost and strayed
away, exceedingly his glory grew.
Did not even the wisest people trade
mouths for ears? And wasn't the house like new

with his young voice? Ah, surely
hundreds of times she'd had to quench her joy
in him, lest it gleam forth. And all amazed
she followed the boy.

But when, beyond all foresight, at that feast
the wedding guests were left without a wine,
she looked at him and begged him for a gesture
and did not understand the sign

as he protested. Then suddenly it befell:
he did it. Later on she realized
how she was forcing him to miracles
that he worked now, and the whole sacrifice

(Continued on page 27)

VON DER HOCHZEIT ZU KANA—*Continued*

unaufhaltsam. Ja, es stand geschrieben.
Aber war es damals schon bereit?
Sie: sie hatte es herbeigetrieben
in der Blindheit ihrer Eitelkeit.

An dem Tisch voll Früchten und Gemüsen
freute sie sich mit und sah nicht ein,
dass das Wasser ihrer Tränendrüsen
Blut geworden war mit diesem Wein.

OF THE WEDDING AT CANA—*Continued*

was irresistibly predetermined. Yea,
written—but prepared sufficiently?
Yet she had made it come to pass this way
in the very blindness of her vanity.

At the table full of herbs and fruits,
rejoicing with the rest, she had not understood
that the water of her tears at their deep roots
had been transmuted with this wine to blood.

VOR DER PASSION

O HAST du dies gewollt, du hättest nicht
durch eines Weibes Leib entspringen dürfen:
Heilande muss man in den Bergen schürfen,
wo man das Harte aus dem Harten bricht.

Tut dirs nicht selber leid, dein liebes Tal
so zu verwüsten? Siehe meine Schwäche;
ich habe nichts als Milch- und Tränenbäche,
und du warst immer in der Überzahl.

Mit solchem Aufwand wardst du mir verheissen.
Was tratst du nicht gleich wild aus mir hinaus?
Wenn du nur Tiger brauchst, dich zu zerreissen,
warum erzog man mich im Frauenhaus,

ein weiches reines Kleid für dich zu weben,
darin nicht einmal die geringste Spur
von Naht dich drückt—: so war mein ganzes Leben,
und jetzt verkehrst du plötzlich die Natur.

BEFORE THE PASSION

Oʜ, if you wished this, you ought not have dared
to issue forth from any woman's loins;
saviors should be hewn from mountain-mines
in which the hard is broken from the hard.

Are you yourself not sorry thus to make
a desert of your own dear valley? See
my weakness: I have only brooks of milk
and tears. But you were more than sufficiency.

So richly it was promised I should bear you—
why didn't you fiercely burst from me and leave?
If you need only tigers to break and tear you,
why was I reared in the women's house, to weave

and make for you a soft clean swaddling-gown
in which was not the smallest seam to chafe
your body? Even so was my whole life—
now suddenly you twist nature upside down.

PIETÀ

JETZT wird mein Elend voll, und namenlos
erfüllt es mich. Ich starre, wie des Steins
Inneres starrt.
Hart wie ich bin, weiss ich nur Eins:
Du wurdest gross—
... und wurdest gross,
um als zu grosser Schmerz
ganz über meines Herzens Fassung
hinauszustehn.
Jetzt liegst du quer durch meinen Schooss,
jetzt kann ich dich nicht mehr
gebären.

PIETÀ

Now is my misery full. Unutterably
it fills me. I am numb, as stone
is numb inside.
Hard as I am, only one thing I know:
You grew
... and grew,
as if on purpose to stand forth
as agony too vast
for my heart to seize and hold.
Now you lie across my lap—
now I can no more
give birth to you.

STILLUNG MARIÄ MIT DEM
AUFERSTANDENEN

Was sie damals empfanden: ist es nicht
vor allen Geheimnissen süss
und immer noch irdisch:
da er, ein wenig blass noch vom Grab,
erleichtert zu ihr trat:
an allen Stellen erstanden.
O zu ihr zuerst. Wie waren sie da
unaussprechlich in Heilung.
Ja, sie heilten, das wars. Sie hatten nicht nötig,
sich stark zu berühren.
Er legte ihr eine Sekunde
kaum seine nächstens
ewige Hand an die frauliche Schulter.
Und sie begannen
still wie die Bäume im Frühling,
unendlich zugleich,
diese Jahreszeit
ihres äussersten Umgangs.

CONSOLATION OF MARY WITH THE
RESURRECTED CHRIST

WHAT they then felt—is it not sweet
above all secrets
and yet an earthly, human thing,
that he, a little pale still from the tomb,
went toward her, disburdened,
wholly resurrected?
Oh, first to her. How they were then
being healed unspeakably.
Yes, they were healing. That was it.
They did not need to touch each other firmly.
Barely an instant
he laid his soon-to-be-eternal hand
upon the womanly shoulder.
And they began,
silently as trees in spring,
infinitely together,
this season of their uttermost communion.

VOM TODE MARIÄ

I

Dᴇʀsᴇʟʙᴇ grosse Engel, welcher einst
ihr der Gebärung Botschaft niederbrachte,
stand da, abwartend, dass sie ihn beachte,
und sprach: Jetzt wird es Zeit, dass du erscheinst.
Und sie erschrak wie damals und erwies
sich wieder als die Magd, ihn tief bejahend.
Er aber strahlte, und unendlich nahend,
schwand er wie in ihr Angesicht—und hiess
die weithin ausgegangenen Bekehrer
zusammenkommen in das Haus am Hang,
das Haus des Abendmahls. Sie kamen schwerer
und traten bange ein: Da lag, entlang
die schmale Bettstatt, die in Untergang
und Auserwählung rätselhaft Getauchte,
ganz unversehrt, wie eine Ungebrauchte,
und achtete auf englischen Gesang.
Nun da sie alle hinter ihren Kerzen
abwarten sah, riss sie vom Übermass
der Stimmen sich und schenckte noch von Herzen
die beiden Kleider fort, die sie besass,
und hob ihr Antlitz auf zu dem und dem . . .
(o Ursprung namenloser Tränen-Bäche).

(Continued on page 36)

OF THE DEATH OF MARY

I

THE same great angel who had brought
long since those pregnant tidings down to her
stood there, waiting until she took thought
of him, and spoke: It's time that you appear.
And she was frightened as before and showed
herself again the virgin, affirming him.
He neared her infinitely and while he glowed
vanished, as if into her very face—
and bade the Apostles who were far away
to gather at the house upon the slope,
the house of the Last Supper. They
came fearfully with heavy hearts. She lay,
deeply wrapped in mystery, along
the narrow bed, untouched, one not used, thinking
of her election and of this slow sinking,
and listening to the angelic song.
Now when she saw them waiting behind their candles,
she wrested herself above the excess of voices
and gladly gave away both of her mantles,
and turned her face to this and that one there ...
(O springhead of unutterable brooks of tears).

(Continued on page 37)

VOM TODE MARIÄ—*Continued*

Sie aber legte sich in ihre Schwäche
und zog die Himmel an Jerusalem
so nah heran, dass ihre Seele nur,
austretend, sich ein wenig strecken musste:
schon hob er sie, der alles von ihr wusste,
hinein in ihre göttliche Natur.

II

Wer hat bedacht, dass bis zu ihrem Kommen
der viele Himmel unvollständig war?
Der Auferstandne hatte Platz genommen,
doch neben ihm, durch vierundzwanzig Jahr,
war leer der Sitz. Und sie begannen schon
sich an die reine Lücke zu gewöhnen,
die wie verheilt war, denn mit seinem schönen
Hinüberscheinen füllte sie der Sohn.

So ging auch sie, die in die Himmel trat,
nicht auf ihn zu, so sehr es sie verlangte;
dort war kein Platz, nur Er war dort und prangte
mit einer Strahlung, die ihr wehe tat.
Doch da sie jetzt, die rührende Gestalt,
sich zu den neuen Seligen gesellte
und unauffällig, licht zu licht, sich stellte,
da brach aus ihrem Sein ein Hinterhalt
von solchem Glanz, dass der von ihr erhellte
Engel geblendet aufschrie: Wer ist die?

(Continued on page 38)

OF THE DEATH OF MARY—*Continued*

Again she sank back in her weakness, drawing
the heavens down, so near Jerusalem
that her soul, which was already going,
had but to stretch itself a little—for he
who knew full well about her was even then
raising her to her divinity.

II

Who has considered that till she appeared
the many heavens were still incomplete?
The resurrected one had taken his seat,
but next to him, for four and twenty years,
the place was empty. And they had begun
to feel that the clean gap there had been healed,
for beautifully, long since, it had been filled
by the overstreaming radiance of the Son.

So even she, who entered heaven, went
not toward him, although her heart was fain;
there was no room, for He was there, resplendent
in an aureole that gave her pain.
But now when she, the touching figure, joined
the newly blessèd ones, light unto light,
unostentatiously, and took her seat,
burst suddenly from her being such long-pent
glory, the angel she made radiant
and dazzled cried out: Who is she?

(Continued on page 39)

VOM TODE MARIÄ—*Continued*

Ein Staunen war. Dann sahn sie alle, wie
Gott-Vater oben unsern Herrn verhielt,
so dass, von milder Dämmerung umspielt,
die leere Stelle wie ein wenig Leid
sich zeigte, eine Spur von Einsamkeit,
wie etwas, was er noch ertrug, ein Rest
irdischer Zeit, ein trockenes Gebrest—.
Man sah nach ihr: sie schaute ängstlich hin,
weit vorgeneigt, als fühlte sie: i c h bin
sein längster Schmerz—: und stürtzte plötzlich vor.
Die Engel aber nahmen sie zu sich
und stützten sie und sangen seliglich
und trugen sie das letzte Stück empor.

III

Doch vor dem Apostel Thomas, der
kam, da es zu spät war, trat der schnelle
längst darauf gefasste Engel her
und befahl an der Begräbnisstelle:

Dräng den Stein beiseite. Willst du wissen,
wo die ist, die dir das Herz bewegt:
Sieh: sie ward wie ein Lavendelkissen
eine Weile da hineingelegt,

(Concluded on page 40)

OF THE DEATH OF MARY—*Continued*

All were amazed. Then they saw verily
how Father-God was holding back our Lord
so that the empty place, by dusk obscured,
seemed like a little grief,
a touch of loneliness to be endured,
the scab of a drying canker, like a brief
remnant of earth-time. They gazed and she
was watching, leaning far out, anxiously,
as if she felt: *I* am his longest pain—
then suddenly fell forward.
But among themselves the angels bore
her up and singing beatifically
carried her farther on, one last piece more.

III

But before Thomas the Apostle, come
too late, strode swiftly forth the angel who
was long prepared for this, and bade them do
whatever should be done about the tomb.

Roll the stone aside. Would you know where
she is now who has so moved your heart:
Behold, for a short while she was laid in there,
like a little pillow of lavender,

(Concluded on page 41)

VOM TODE MARIÄ—*Concluded*

dass die Erde künftig nach ihr rieche
in den Falten wie ein feines Tuch.
Alles Tote (fühlst du), alles Sieche
ist betäubt von ihrem Wohlgeruch.

Schau den Leinwand: wo ist eine Bleiche,
wo er blendend wird und geht nicht ein?
Dieses Licht aus dieser reinen Leiche
war ihm klärender als Sonnenschein.

Staunst du nicht, wie sanft sie ihm entging?
Fast als wär sie's noch, nichts ist verschoben.
Doch die Himmel sind erschüttert oben:
Mann, knie hin und sieh mir nach und sing.

OF THE DEATH OF MARY—*Concluded*

so that the earth may smell, in time to come,
of her among its folds, like a rich shawl.
All death (you feel this), all
sickness are overpowered by her perfume.

Behold the linen shroud! What bleacher's work
could, without shrinkage, yield such dazzling white?
This light streaming from the immaculate corpse
made it more pure than could the full sunlight.

Do you not marvel how quietly she left?
You'd think that she were still in the smooth weft.
Yet the high heavens there are shuddering:
man, kneel down, gaze after me and sing.

NOTES

NOTES

Geburt Mariä, pp. 2–3:

Concerning the parents of the Virgin Mary, if we were to obey the admonition of St. Peter Damian, "we should consider it a blameable and needless curiosity to inquire about those things that the Evangelists did not deem it advisable to relate." The *Catholic Encyclopedia* (VIII, 406) states that the tradition rests on the apocryphal "Gospel of James" (i.e., the "Protoevangelium Jacobi") and the Pseudo-Matthew, and (I, 538) condenses a beautiful version from the "Protoevangelium." Tischendorf's *Evangelia apocrypha* (Leipzig, 1876), which includes in Greek the "Protoevangelium" and in Latin the Pseudo-Matthew, the "De nativitate Mariae," and the "Historia Josephi," was as readily available to Rilke as it is to us. Volume V of Luzac's Semitic Text and Translation Series (London, 1889) presents much of the same material in English, in a translation by E. A. Wallis Budge of a Syriac version of the apocryphal books; the reader of the present volume may follow the story there, if he doesn't care to wrestle with Greek and Latin. Joachim and Hannah, we learn, were rich, pious, and childless. The husband was not permitted to sacrifice at the Temple, on the grounds that men without offspring were unworthy to be admitted.... He went into the mountains to complain to God in solitude, and Hannah prayed tearfully to be freed from the curse of sterility. In due time, angels appeared to both suppliants and assured them that their prayers would be answered. One legend asserts that Hannah (Anne) was ninety years old at the time.

Three of the German words in this short poem are difficult to translate: *Verdichtung, Getue,* and *klugte.* The first has a technical meaning: tension, precipitation. The second is colloquial; one must risk a misreading of "what was doing." And the last word literally means "acted wise—pretended to know it all." Yet these go off with admirable smoothness in the original. The delightful incident of the futile old man's stilling the cow is apparently the poet's own invention. But it is hard to work in a cow's mooing in so tensely religious a poem.

THE LIFE OF THE VIRGIN MARY

Die Darstellung Mariä im Tempel, pp. 4–7:

The "Protoevangelium Jacobi" (vii–viii) and the "De nativitate
Mariae" (Tischendorf, *Evangelia apocrypha,* pp. 14–17, 117–179)
agree that the parents, faithful to a vow they had promised to fulfill
if they should have a child, presented Mary in the Temple when she
was but three years old, and that she mounted the great steps unac-
companied and made, at that time, voluntary vows of virginity. Other
apocryphal writings, for instance, the "Christus patiens" of Pseudo-
Gregory of Nazianzen (Migne, *Patres graeci,* XXXVIII, 244), agree
in general that the child remained in the Temple to be educated and
that she enjoyed holy visions and daily visits from the angels. When
she was fourteen the high priest wanted to send her home to be mar-
ried, but she reminded him sternly of her vow. In his embarrassment
he consulted with God. It was in accordance with the celestial advice
that he called together the young men of the family of David and
promised the girl in marriage to him whose staff should become a
resting place for the Holy Ghost in the form of a dove. It was Joseph
who was divinely empowered to manifest the proper miraculous
foliation and who subsequently became the bridegroom.

There are many impressive paintings of the subject, principally by
the Venetians, who loved to present scenes of splendor. Titian's is the
most happily conceived, and the little girl, as she mounts the steps
alone, toward the great portals where the "threatening one" awaits,
sparkling with jewels (the Urim and Thummim mentioned half a
dozen times in the Old Testament), is one of the most majestic yet
strangely pathetic child figures I have ever seen. Rilke, however,
prefers to stress an imaginary architectural landscape which gives the
reader a vista of such vastness and mystery that the mind carries a
borrowed sense of grandeur over and applies it to the girl. But really,
she is impressive enough in her own person and needs no such gran-
diose trimmings. Only Mantegna could have painted this unreal
landscape of arches and pillars in space.

The *C. E.* (XV, 464G) says that Jewish girls were considered mar-
riageable at the age of twelve years and six months, and that after
the betrothal the bride did not live with the groom "until about a
year later," when the marriage was celebrated. "Mary trusted the

THE LIFE OF THE VIRGIN MARY

Divine guidance implicitly, and thus was certain that her vow would be kept even in her married state."

The use of the second person in this poem immediately enlists the reader and makes him an actual spectator.

Mariä Verkündigung, pp. 8–9:

According to Luke, 1:35, Gabriel made the announcement: "The Holy Ghost shall come upon thee, and the power of the Highest shall overshadow thee: therefore also that holy thing which shall be born of thee shall be called the Son of God."

The charming parenthetical interlude of the conception of the unicorn demands documentation. Brand's *Popular Antiquities of Great Britain* (London, Reeves & Turner, 1905), pp. 605–606, ascribes the earliest mention of this animal—not to be confused with the monoceros in the Bible—to the *Bestiary* of Philip de Thaun, where it is asserted that the beast was highly dangerous to anyone except a virgin. The *Archaeological Album* (ed. Thomas Wright, London, 1845) says that the beast "became tame in the presence of a pure virgin," and translates Philip's account of how it might be caught. If a virgin will wait alone and patiently in the greenwood until a specimen chances by, it will immediately lay its head in her lap, and if she happens to have a piece of string and keeps her presence of mind, she can tie the beast and lead it back to town. Such a procedure must have been more difficult than it seems on the face of it, for I have discovered only two unicorn horns in captivity: the one in the Musée de Cluny in Paris is about six feet long and has spiral convolutions; that in the famous Buckhorn Collection in San Antonio, Texas—of all places!—resembles the straightened tusk of a young elephant; it has no spiral markings and is about four feet long. Perhaps we have here to do with two different species. There may even have been an American variety, but to date this seems the only one which has allowed itself to be captured. Robert Brown's *The Unicorn: A Mythological Investigation* (London, 1881) and Charles Gould's *Mythical Monsters* (London, 1886) present enough material for a doctoral thesis on this fascinating subject, though it is to be doubted that any student would make happier use of his learning than Professor Odell Shepard has done in *The Lore of the Unicorn* (Boston,

Houghton Mifflin, 1930). Even in this humdrum world, willing as I am to believe in miracles, I find great difficulty in stomaching Rilke's alleged parthenogenetic conception of the animal.

One of his *Sonnets to Orpheus* (II, 4) presents a poetic vision of the unicorn (which I translate):

> Oh, this is the animal that never was.
> They did not know it, and for all that
> they loved his neck, his posture, and his gait,
> clean to the great eyes with their silent gaze.
>
> Really, he never *was*. But since they loved
> him, the pure creature grew. And they left space
> always for him: an unencumbered place
> where he need scarce be real as his head moved,
>
> lightly tossing. Him they fed no corn,
> but ever the possibility that he might
> exist, which gave the beast such strength he bore
>
> a horn from his broad forehead. Just one horn.
> Unto a virgin he appeared, all white,
> and was in the silver mirror and in her.

He also used this material in his *Malte* where he described the famous tapestries in the Musée de Cluny, "La Dame à la Licorne."

How different the picture of the angel and the maid is from that painted by Simone Martini (in the Uffizi), about which we read:

> What keen-eyed hawk with fierce wings, golden-flecked,
> swoops in this room which straightway blossoms light,
> as if a comet burst and burned the night?
> And what swift help can sweep in to protect
>
> the blest and doomed girl who draws back in fear
> before the voice whose awful visible words
> could swirl the wisest virgin off her guard
> into the apotheosis of fire?

Mariä Heimsuchung, pp. 10–11:

The *C. E.* (XV, 464G) says, on the authority of St. Ambrose (Migne, *Patres latini*, XV, 1560), that Mary "determined to add to the pleasure of her pious relative"; and Luke, 1:39, tells that she "went into the hill country with haste into a city of Juda." But a half-dozen other locations have been suggested by various writers. Luke, 1:5–25, gives the story of the parents of John the Baptist, and further, in verse 36, we find the annunciation of his birth: "And, behold, thy cousin Elisabeth, she hath also conceived a son in her old age: and this is the sixth month with her, who was called barren." Verse 37: "For with God nothing shall be impossible." Verse 41 continues: "And it came to pass, that, when Elisabeth heard the salutation of Mary, the babe leaped in her womb; and Elisabeth was filled with the Holy Ghost."

Stanza 3 is a wonderful description of that womanly weakness incident to the condition in which the two women miraculously found themselves. And they "swayed toward one another and touched each other's garments and hair." Few poets could have written that, full as it is of human gestures which lie too deep for words. It is no wonder that women like Rilke.

Argwohn Josephs, pp. 12–13:

I can do nothing better in documentation of this poem than to quote fully the origin of its inspiration, from Matthew, 1:18–20: "Now the birth of Jesus Christ was on this wise: When as his mother Mary was espoused to Joseph, before they came together, she was found with the child of the Holy Ghost. Then Joseph her husband, being a just man, and not willing to make her a publick example, was minded to put her away privily. But while he thought on these things, behold, the angel of the Lord appeared unto him in a dream, saying, Joseph, thou son of David, fear not to take unto thee Mary thy wife: for that which is conceived within her is of the Holy Ghost." Rilke gives this a modern but not irreverent psychological slant in having the angel use occupational terms in order to convince the carpenter. He has humanized both the husband and the angel. And it is a fine close when the man pushes back his workman's cap and bursts into song.

Verkündigung über den Hirten, pp. 14–17:

From Luke, 2:8–10: "And there were in the same country shepherds abiding in the fields, keeping watch over their flock by night.

And, lo, the angel of the Lord came upon them, and the glory of the Lord shone around about them: and they were sore afraid. And the angel said unto them, Fear not: for, behold, I bring you good tidings of great joy, which shall be to all people." In my antepenultimate line, "recórd" must be given the proper pronunciation and accentuation.

Rast aus der Flucht in Ägypten, pp. 20–23:

This flight was occasioned by the angel's warning after Herod had sent the wise men to Bethlehem to find out the meaning of the star. Although they did not return to inform him, an angel appeared to Joseph in a dream (Matthew, 2:13), saying: "Arise and take the young child and his mother, and flee into Egypt, and be thou there until I bring thee word."

The *C. E.* (XV, 465) has a reference in point—and strangely timely it seems, after almost two thousand years: "Persecuted Jews had ever sought a refuge in Egypt. . . . about the time of Christ Jewish colonists were especially numerous in the land of the Nile. . . . it required a journey of at least ten days from Bethlehem to reach the habitable districts of Egypt." Cf. I Kings, 11:40; II Kings, 25:26; Matthew, 2:14; and see Jullien's *L'Égypte* (Lille, 1891), pp. 241–251, and his *L'Arbre de la Vierge à Matariéh* (4th ed., Cairo, 1904). I was finally led to consult the *Standard Cyclopedia* (III, 1233–1234: "The sycamore of the ancients was a kind of fig known as Pharaoh's fig, *Ficus sycomorus.*" Baedeker's *Egypt* (p. 129) assures us that this incident mentioned in the poem occurred in Matariyeh, a town in lower Egypt, five miles north of Cairo. The tree is still in existence, as is the spring made to flow by Christ. The spring is not brackish, as are the others in the district. It was used by Mary for washing the child's clothes. Then Baedeker gravely concludes, "The tree was planted subsequent to 1672."

My credulity about the poet's accuracy in introducing a mule into the episode—an animal never painted, as far as I know, by the Italians who treated the subject—sent me to the *Encylopedia Americana* (1946 ed., XIX, 553), which says: "Mules have been known from the earliest ages; there are frequent references to them in Scripture." At that, I consider it exceedingly unwise to entrust a young mother and child to the back of a beast which is notoriously intransigent, and which would, moreover, require three times the amount of food, a scarce item in a desert country. An ass, however, can eat a handful of rolled oats and travel all day.

In Budge's translation of "The History of the Virgin Mary" (Luzac, Vol. V, as mentioned above, pp. 55–58) we find an episode entitled "Story of the Young Man Who Had Been Turned into a Mule." Briefly, the story is this. The Holy Family, fleeing into Egypt, meet with some young women who, though showing signs of deep private distress, offer hospitality for a night. They politely refrain from telling their guests the cause of their grief, but to Mary's servant they explain that a fine mule which they have decked with silken trappings and fed with sesame is actually their brother, who has been metamorphosed by a sorceress. The upshot is that Mary sets the Child on the mule's back and calls upon His power to make the beast a man again, whereupon the young women's brother resumes his proper shape. This is astonishingly remindful of Apuleius' immortal *Golden Ass;* the story must be even older than the *Metamorphoses* of Lucius of Patrae, upon which the African-born Apuleius drew.

Besides the "quiet tree" in stanza 5, there are several other friendly trees in the stories about the Virgin, for instance, the cherry tree which bent down its fruit to Mary as she passed, and the holly tree which sprouted suddenly a great thicket with thorny leaves which prevented Herod's soldiers from making a thorough search for the runaways.

Von der Hochzeit zu Kana, pp. 24–27:

This miracle is factually described in John, 2:6–10: "And there were set there six waterpots of stone, after the manner of purifying of the Jews, containing two or three firkins apiece. Jesus saith unto them, Fill the waterpots with water. And they filled them up to the brim. And he saith unto them, Draw out now, and bear unto the governor of the feast. And they bare it. When the ruler of the feast had tasted the water that was made wine, and knew not whence it was: (but the servants which drew the water knew;) the governor called the bridegroom, and saith unto him, Every man at the beginning doth set forth good wine; and when men have well drunk, then that which is worse: but thou hast kept the good wine until now."

There is nothing irreverent in the last stanza, in which the poet performs a lesser and mortal miracle when he lets the tears of mother love actually participate in the transmutation which goes even further than that in the story.

I hope I may be forgiven, as a Scot, for having computed that the amount of wine thus produced—and I have taken as an average two and one-half firkins, at the probable English valuation when the King James version was made—was around 150 gallons, which ought to have been adequate for quite a celebration.

The intensely human action of the mother who wants her son to put his better foot forward, to shine in the company, is another example of the poet's delicate understanding when he was dealing with women (in literature).

Vor der Passion, pp. 28–29:

Here again we have a speech of Mary as mother of a son, forgetting completely for the time her mission as the mother of a savior, which is a far more arduous calling. Throughout the poem it is the physical aspect of her suffering that she stresses: the actual birth, the suckling, and finally her woman's work as a weaver of the famous robe. There is a legend that it was made for the newborn Child, and that as He grew to manhood it increased in size, *pari passu.* In the New Testament, it is mentioned in John, 19:23–24: "Then the soldiers, when they had crucified Jesus, took his garments, and made four parts, to every soldier a part; and also his coat: now the coat was without seam, woven from the top throughout. They said therefore among themselves, Let us not rend it, but cast lots for it, whose it shall be: that the scripture might be fulfilled, which saith, They parted my raiment among them, and for my vesture they did cast lots. These things therefore the soldiers did." The other three Gospels do not specifically discuss the seamless garment.

Concerning this remarkable robe, *tunica inconsutilis,* the *Catholic Encyclopedia* (VII, 400–402) says that it was authenticated by the "Sylvester Diploma" of Pope Sylvester, which was addressed to the church of Trier. It was of "a plain brownish coloured fabric to all appearances linen or cotton." In 1890–91, further investigation determined successfully the authenticity of the garment; the results "furnished no reason to doubt the ancient tradition of Trier." Helena, the mother of the Emperor Constantine, brought it to Trier (Trèves) soon after 306 A.D. It was later enshrined in the cathedral treasury, in a glass case. In 1939 I was happy to be able to substantiate personally, reverently, and not like a doubting Thomas, this miracle. And I was allowed to compare (through the glass) the official measurements. The fabric is about 1.56 m. in front length, with the back about 0.8 m. longer. The shoulder width is about 0.72 m. and the bottom width about 1.15 m. It looks as if it had been woven of camel and goat hair. It is naturally a faded brownish white, weather-stained. The edges of the sleeve ends, neck, and bottom are hemmed and are stitched with very fine seams. The probable number of threads per inch in this finely woven garment would be about 100. Helena was also fortunate enough to be able to discover some pieces of the Cross, but these were apparently sent otherwhere for use as dedicatory relics for other churches.

Pietà, pp. 30–31:

The Italian title and the exact picture given make it undoubtedly the poetic reverie of the Virgin in the famous statue by Michelangelo in Saint Peter's. This is one of his most delicately conceived and tenderly executed works. The usual vigor and energy of his figures is of course completely absent. The son is a young man in his physical prime, but Mary is represented as a woman of about twenty-five, with a very beautiful and unlined face. The grief in the face is expressed without the use of ordinary devices—contortion of the features and gestures. The very stone may be said to be taking part in the sorrow: it is marble coming to life in human agony. The German text has only five rhyme words, but there are several almost inaudible inner rhymes, sometimes concealed in a word. I have not been able to duplicate this effect.

Stillung Mariä mit dem Auferstandenen, pp. 32–33:

It is the Gospel of St. Luke again which gives me assurance that Rilke was on the right track here. In chapter 24 the evangelist writes that the women who return to the tomb of Christ meet two men "in shining garments" who tell them that Christ has risen. Later, in verse

36, He appears before his disciples, shows them His wounds, and asks, in verse 41: "Have ye here any meat?" 42: "And they gave him a piece of broiled fish, and of an honeycomb." 43: "And he took it, and did eat before them."

In John, chapter 20, it is Mary Magdalene to whom Christ appears, in verse 14. And in verse 17 he utters the famous *Noli me tangere* of the Vulgate.

Notice what an artist Rilke is here. Contrary to the uses of many of the painters, he shows none of the wounds left by the crown of thorns, the whip, the lance, or the nails. This is a splendid and unmelodramatic restraint. Jesus is merely "a little pale still from the tomb." It is a characteristic avoidance of excess on the poet's part; cf. his *Duineser Elegien*, II:

> Erstaunte euch nicht auf attischen Stelen die Vorsicht
> menschlicher Geste? war nicht Liebe und Abschied
> so leicht auf die Schultern gelegt, als wär es aus anderen
> Stoffe gemacht als bei uns?

> (Were you not astonished by the caution of human gestures
> on the Attic stelae? Were not love and parting
> so lightly laid on the shoulders, as if they were made
> of other stuff than with us?)

This seems to me to be almost the same delicate gesture of the present poem.

Vom Tode Mariä (Drei Stücke), pp. 34–41:

We read in the *C. E.* (XV, 471) that Mary's death was not the result of disease, "from which she was exempt. . . . Her passing away is a sacrifice of love completing the dolorous sacrifice of her life. It is the death in the kiss of the Lord (*in osculo Domini*), of which the just die." Apollonius, from whom this was taken, concludes that her death occurred in 48 A.D. Her Assumption into Heaven has been treated in the *Zeitschrift für katholische Theologie* (1906), pp. 210 sqq. Of course, it has been painted hundreds of times, always with settings duplicating the splendor of some mighty emperor's court; it couldn't be painted in the spiritualized fashion which Rilke is fortunate enough to lend it.

I—p. 34: There are a dozen versions and opinions as to where the Virgin died. Present limitations of space, and inconclusiveness of these documents, make inadvisable even a summary. I am particularly impressed by Rilke's intuitive gentleness when he mentions her remembering to give away her clothes.

II—p. 36: If she died twenty-four years after her son, the date would be approximately ten years later than that given by Apollonius. The filling in of the complete·hierarchy of Heaven by the Virgin's death is handled here in a masterful fashion. But I am unhappy about that figure of the "drying canker," which certainly has no place in such a glorious description. It is a fine touch to have her not quite able to come that "last piece" alone.

III—p. 38: The Apostle Thomas seems to have been particularly active in these posthumous caretakings. That Mary did leave her tomb was substantiated somewhat later by the report of Juvenal, Bishop of Jerusalem, to the Emperor Marcion. The emperor, wishing to consecrate a new church in Constantinople, asked that the body of the Virgin be sent. The good prelate, however, "cited an ancient tradition saying that the sacred body had been assumed in Heaven, and sent only the coffin and the winding sheet." (*C. E.,* XV, 471.) The final image of the poem, the impression left by the body in the grave-clothes, is very human and haunting—for who has not gazed sadly at the last imprint left by a beloved head on a pillow? Rilke always knows how to wring one last spasm of feeling from his reader.

He mentioned in his correspondence that his *Marienleben* was only a slight thing, but that he would "always get on well with it." It is certainly one of the most succinct and delicately written of the many lives of the Virgin Mary.

20534   6/18